Gender City

Other works by Lisa Samuels include:

LETTERS (Meow Press 1996)
The Seven Voices (O Books 1998)
War Holdings (Pavement Saw Press 2003)
Paradise for Everyone (Shearsman Books 2005)
Increment (a family romance) (Bronze Skull Press 2006)
The Invention of Culture (Shearsman Books 2008)
Throe (Oystercatcher Press 2009)
Tomorrowland (Shearsman Books 2009)
Mama Mortality Corridos (Holloway Press 2010)
Anti M (Chax Press 2011)

Lisa Samuels

Gender City

Shearsman Books

First published in the United Kingdom in 2011 by
Shearsman Books Ltd
58 Velwell Road
Exeter EX4 4LD

www.shearsman.com

ISBN 978-1-84861-169-6

Copyright © Lisa Samuels, 2011.

The right of Lisa Samuels to be identified as the author of this work
has been asserted by her in accordance with the
Copyrights, Designs and Patents Act of 1988.
All rights reserved.

Cover image: Laura McLauchlan, 'Rat Coaxing'
(collage with retinal image by Toby Holmes), © copyright 2011.

Acknowledgements

Thanks to the editors who published excerpts from *Gender City* in
Hambone (Nathaniel Mackey), *Jacket* (Pam Brown),
The Other Room Anthology 09/10 (James Davies, Tom Jenks, & Scott Thurston),
and *Veer Off* (Stephen Mooney).

Contents

1. Homosocial fugue	9
2. Love song: the city	19
3. Immanent domain	28
4. Blood on the tracks	39
5. The Prison-house	50
6. Exodus	65
7. Kit out	79
8. The Barbie Doll museum	89
9. The film version	99

The most pleasing civic object would be erotic hope. What could be more beautiful than to compile it with our minds, converting complicity to synthesis? A synthetics of space improvises unthought shape. Suppose we no longer call it identity. Spatial synthetics cease to enumerate how we have failed. Enough dialectical stuttering. We propose a theoretical device that amplifies the cognition of thresholds. It would add to the body the vertiginously unthinkable. That is, a pavilion.

>   —Lisa Robertson,
>   *Occasional Work and Seven Walks
>   from the Office for Soft Architecture*

The front entrance to the pavilion is a welcoming veranda, a lofty canopy supported by a forest of pillars interspersed with shorter pou (pillars), many of them interactive, providing shelter for visitors watching cultural performances and queuing for entry to the interior.

>   —The New Zealand Pavilion,
>   New Zealand at Shanghai World Expo 2010

1 Homosocial fugue

All I have or all I want
are sight words in this town
where the gentle modesty of afternoon
precedes the blanks of morning, when
our circuitry is prodded with hellos

Those who live here are divest
        PRINT MANUFACTURING ROSE
        TYPES GENTLY PLACED COLLOQUIAL
on the paper beaches by the binding
shore, feet hooligans tracing
a length of separation
    I'VE FOLDED THE IMMODESTY TO CLAY FORMS
        NEAR MY ELECTRIC BED
wherein the liquid certainty transfixes
    MUCH MORE RAPID THAN FORMER
    UNCONDITIONALS WERE KNOWN FOR

      weeping or gnashing of wires
        of gone items mentioned
     of the strange arithmetic of discomfiture

  turning each specific happening into a play
  next door my head, a chorus of low electric birds
  a mile away at the square

Here comes someone who thinks he has a point of view
you might enjoy, loud and louder, your resupplier
of the modern. The man grimaces
with the lips of the newly sane

  we turn tail waiting for you, we turn coat
    but the larger project is a breach
    of confidence same same, another
    small chapter in the very large
    book of suicide. Inside or insight
       a t shirt with the realm of defamiliarisation
       to itself. A brute economy forward

you laugh, but if the goal is
embedded, how will I find you?
Pin text to all your clothes
                THEY UNDERESTIMATE THE STRICT
                REPENTANCE OF THE PAST POINT
waiting, strayed between. He walked as though
hot coals were tender motive.

  Underneath the arch we huddle
  the immediacy of speaking ceasing

  quietly the sea rushes the sky
    makes whooshing lightly the body of
the stranger appeals to us
    it heaves a little and breathes
  underneath its basic quietude

  the sea rushes the sky makes little sounds
  under the stranger we look to see
the vanishing conversation we all heard

    MINE EYES WERE YOURS, YOUR HANDS ARE MINE
    WITHIN CUSP AND WITHOUT
        WE SOLACED WITH OUR CURFEW MOUTHS

    the heavy coastal friction masked
    against our wired shores

it tries to overtake us and we bank it
all forthwith
        dirigible unflowerings
          connected for our bouts
    the sails are up, the wind is strong
      we blow it with our lungs
    we've turned into the forces
      we were punted
        lexicon

The stranger joins us presently
at the cellophane placed temperate
on the panels of our hands

we want the stranger to be us we want
to be the trim that coastals all the brace
against the trouble that we're

AMBIENT FIT

FAIR LIGHT

WHALE LIT AIR

RIGHT TO OUR EYE

WAYS FLICK

YOUR CAUSAL RET

NOR REEL IN TRI

PART VEST WE

UNCONCEAL WE SWORE

ING PLUCK

YOUR HEART STRINGS FELT

ON SCORE LILT HEARS

NO BIRD NOR

SHUCKS YOUR CO

(very much like we can't know
what bumped against us softly
in the crowded night of ideas)

   you belong to gender I knew that before we arrived and so
it's no surprise an expedition as not needed to prove
but our material images are waking early if anything

centre prinking on chairs weighing their personal
idem, speaking heliotrope Glaswegian tagalong
speaking in perfume frequently islandic the
lingua hysterica we've just now heard

       (it was early morning before the break of dark
       we rose from our modified bandanas

         to put on the bus the modified terrain distress
          of marginal retainers standing in a line about
         the distal reproduction of said cages

        and rents excruciating conscious while the bones
         sighed for the annihilation of architecture)
nothing like that could ever happen here

the least opportune domestics have their taps
intact heroic things inhabit not-bad franchise
art nor folded sumptuous, minute from before

a hint of undulant dash on slope, a tribal
launch on pose still writhes with truck I take
one with me and another when I go

to get the rocks and nails for my own filmic
resolution monitors, interregnum smiles
at the camera given magnitude by

our very own lab neighbors growing
cowboys, in all events taken
   in melody within and without smiling

(for details see the ghost of the man)
walking up the street arm in arm with
   the book he always wanted to be

What evening am I in? search for the white
                ladder inside the ground inscribing
        vocative, monument

Why am I listening
            patiently while go his self-made stones
           supple with the opacity of the grave
      that touches   heart's own temperature

        sweet child of the bays and dollies
        seated on the prime
       solicitude its own dire need for design
for the torpid old man his whimsy

born into a daunting surety that
           no one reveres habitués, they can always
      find you smiling inapplicable
     to the novice trend of instinct

We've come to like the little brain
the tapestries all heart
maybe the queen is on our lap
and milks about to start
SELF-CONSCIOUS WITHOUT LOVE EXACTLY
ludic over basic language states
the distribution is like the music

WE DECIDED
TO KNOW OF THE LIFE OF THE TONGUE
not flicking its
rights but more of an impulse

ink saliva scattered on the local animals
whose names we know though tattered
in ambrosia tats (even with the parapets
we strive from)

Founder
with his salt gasps barely functioning
holding the edge of the furniture in order
REPUBLICANIZED IN ENORMOUS
CONSEQUENCE WE'RE HERE FOR
YOUR PECULIAR SELF-IMAGINARY

      to translate the person
      with an enormous barrel of sand, the salt
      crunching down beautifully on his immanence

 Bewinged there with her alter
petticoats she was withering
  jeans, titillating the bloody
hounds of offering he was roped to

she resembling lollipops of THE NATURAL LAND
front borders made quite low and aspect shade
in the center scent we carry
 on to give more fabulous infill
     shape and reason to feel differential
pardon, some rein

    we put the bit in our teeth and chomp hard
    down on wagon wheels, on wheelwrights
      whose enthusiastics carry
     swallowed time

2 Love song: the city

In this separation and distance we can hardly be called unknown
with our lock-ons and our travesties
with pink frills all abounding

you having laid the architecture perfectly for such routs
hardly screen the piece
by demolition of originary
struts, whilst our arms entwining
reach the ideology we strive for

    Meanwhile passers by
are full of rancor bubbles (having wasted tiny rations for
              an irretrievable sublime we call economy)
though their faces are a mask of story
streams we're swimming in and nearly drown

    EMOTIVE THRILL OF ANTIROAD
   EMBRACES ALL THE CONCRETE PILES
    NOT JUST A DURABLE SALT
              we trothe
  our feet encumbered with   our mouths
  we could allow the goods to throw
   their own corrosive cords right out the window—

 Le Corbusier would have us know
we take our mouths and preach to those
   (still sauntering by with habit acts)
 by roads and windows   ties
   post-wretched equally safe
   acculturated chains like these
   are nothing as compared

   JUST AS THE ALPHA STATE'S A MIME
   AND ONE SUSCEPTIBLE OF JOY
    TALKS GOTHIC WITH AN UNDERWORLD
so we ride out to meet our who

The activists were having fun
though ticking at their hearts
were all mortality's encyclicals
the little portrait they once had
the armaments so glorious when they were
> BOYS TREAD OVEN CLOISTER
> > GIRLS FED PIES TO DOVER
> COUNTENANCE

    they were as all we fed nor asked
       they felt nor all we heated
         in the asphalt corrogations of disarmament—

they meant everything they said and we their listeners
vroomed integrity, which nothing could gainsay
    nor our arms fervently dispute
        THE ROAD
      we felt our eyes enlarge
      our caustic stays fell punitive
     and wreathed with ideation all
    the tentacles outnumbered us
   we joined such groovy raspish ways
       we intimate

'This city with its rampant groves is tilted Amsterdam'
This city with its windy curves
      is piety, its tortured name replaces all our plans

and this one with its grid so fair
makes merry with our stop-and-go
        OUR ARMS HAVE STROPPED THE HOARDS OUR
        REALLY SPATIAL SO NEGOTIATE
    so fair aloft technology
   so fertile with infantile distribution
     a leisure nomad fairly lit
    a postdysfunction skit   a hoard
          a smile we felt
      upon our skin as down we're in

THE SOFT FALL OF THE SIDEWALK
FLATLY GREETS
MY CHEEK A FAIR ANATOMY
THE SCRAPE
 A LIFESTYLE ATTITUDE
THE MOMENTARY LYING THERE
APPOINTMENT MADE WITH ALL ETERNITY

And to the middle of it Trudi strode
to pick one part and hear it speak
a Cyprian ode withal
        material pleasure makes its mark
        her cheek it held the marvel
        spark our eyes fell on the ground
we parked the car.

Convince my knives to cut the tape
we had as willful time
       on skits
FROM THERE before as after nodes no origin
     I'm 'from' there still
  no skirts to tread on
    zealously, nor hair on fire

We're headed out embedded in the cavalcades
  whose edge on froth
  whose nationalistic newness
may be naming the volcanic type that made our reaches
    fetching to a grosser afternoon
 though tired as ashes peaked to fold on sub-time

   ALL THOSE GREENERIES PROVING something
       nameless she can't know
    no western call or host sublime, the roots
  inside the roots a real
   replacement for the arguments
    droll imprimatur keeps
   implicit in the glass slope
  monuments to industrial fusion techniques

For there's THE LAW then there's ALL ELSE
    we're primed on charter   seeing
        the proclamation's a divinosphere
    whose faults lie underneath ideas
WE CAN'T KNOW AS HAVING YET
        we name our sons all Cato, Cook, Columbus
    or da Vinci wheel type casts
or better Gutenbergs whose 'hast thou known me
    literal rose'
will cast us Heine-wards   through dulcet spills
        while we still fodder on?

I CAUGHT HIS HAIR INSIDE MY TEETH
       a magical synecdoche
   for answer turned into a fish in
                (my imagination's rude
                   installs his heart inside the flares
                      I send) my brain to keep
       where dinner times are made for deals
         when social value is exchanged

   HER SWEAT DROPS DOWN INTO THE GENTLE SALAD
            IN HIS BELLY   HAUNTS
                AND WRECKED ASSIZES
       sacrifice rolls through his eyes
          as down the just-made sill he looks
       the mandatory harbor
                         takes a photo
     of his leaning scan
                   imprints it
       on the tumid land so it can grow
            inside his brain   whose greens
             reverse   configure, fallow
      his eyelid shades turn into marrow

    You see we have a task at hand
a city built of argument
explicit for its metal shires
replaceable like brickfront cars
but smoothed and succored with the wares
we bring from offering's cognate tears
no roses no nor doves we are
but writ it is with stars with stars

3 Immanent domain

All the ceremonies were continental and so sank
into the sea by our tough lovelies

they were frames there in the rocks become
architectural, red and blue and green

grins they could not translate burst out circuits
blazing a deeply mysterious cult in the origin of
media, coverage, the improbable continuity of bodies

being more nor rather less reportage hire came to stall
inheritance, fit measurements we all stood
for lines, for mustering we could
stand each other mountains like a princess
lying and the valleys like
a foliage blank for kit

your swaying ideations all blanked out
against the wall of land beneath your feet
therein like wounded trees we
furrow and cane united planting
here with box balls blast with height

    So I said this is about a demi-god
      (we never knew which half)
    who pranced around the value
    system we're rooting for
          WE HAD TO KILL HIM TO GET WHAT WE WANT
    but with aught we think as death surrounds
    plantations credulous, surrender fests
    and all the rank unpeeling of the first
level decision (I'm not here to vouch
        the ghost my friend sedition
        routinized by mirror sparks)
    BECAUSE THAT'S AN AMAZING CONTRADICTION
      toppled on the promontory

  the tongues you spent
to test against   the list we're keeping
     secret until everyone is dead

HOW BIG IS YOUR PAROCHIALISM NOW
WE WONDER
      an exclusive focus on the loins
     and limping short from a
    quiet flip urge
     does it as night
   fell when you're ready just let me know
  everybody's running from the waitlist
    whatever happened to
parallelism

  the shining lights of inconsequent pause
  the bellies happy with themselves
  when no one would need to open the hammer
  and carry it out with you

We're trying to get across
a minimum of words conditioned
with an exigent popularity of Pharisee
designed to redistribute the covert imaginary of
our body state

        DESTROY THE NOTEBOOK NEWS
        HABITUALLY BREAK THE LAW
                      Cyclorama
of the continent without regard (the cyber
      sex mouths waiting patiently
  for it swallow swallow)
                      the last
few decades severally hand sewn.

  The problem no such average succumbing
soft voice tumbling down yes I think
that day in the café with the pink napkins
where he ate the restoration complete

How did they ever lose India

says the moniker with
no mindless flinch, a man
gone round the bend and straight
into the face of his enemy

   much later with the sands and tragedian circling
figure eight forecourt
      hirelings put in a group
to manage all the applicants in question

              he is at the centre of reporting
       the global green across which
           walk tall skeletons
         his knelt face
          grey's inward
      fugue taken to extremes

The talk agenda breaks and seals the same
THERE'S A FACSIMILE FOR YOU
capital walker, slow asker
looking for the origins of palatable grasses

       Officially we were not meant to disperse
            thereafter we all took showers to scrub away
         our novelty

Officially we're not meant
     to crave an exponential portion
  of our hourglass vistas over again
        to hunger so at ma ma's luscious jaw
       to fix ourselves by gunshy premonitions

(to hide behind the trees until we're trees
behind the buildings given names)
         while Trudi's blueprint habit shook
        MY SKULL, SHE SAID
       THIS TIME I FELT MYSELF
       BECOME THAT BUILDING

Promised to the city, it surrendered me
           until I knew that   plenty savage luscious
     by-tending
we moved   **THAT WAS THE YES**
       while Bridge he smiles

  We take that trip over to see what
ruptures show this time the commons
gunning at your windows

We smile back politely but still found
the coat man most forbidding
the longer we stood there with
our boxes of hair
        SOMETIMES TWO STRANDS
        TO MAKE A LENGTH OF PROBITY
        SOMETIMES SIMPLY PROOF WHILE

early pastoralists left their mark

horse power, tweed, agitants for imported

equipment to survive our tenders

flag lengths costed over braids

                our canon tables fret work fell

                inside the book

                WE HID BETWEEN

                THE SYNTAX FRAME

          trucked out I felt

        your skin yield vellum

    shout

                thus monogram **WITHIN**

                OUR BEAUTIES PENITENTIAL

            WIDE we spoke

robes on our hips our needles still

emplaced, the alterations

done most pleasant

wide inside

(don't imagine soundtracks high sustained recurred
sharp notes with doubling effects
like an old voice vibrates several chords
don't imagine an electric car moaning
at a pitch it reaches over
as long as you can hear)
        that camera lucida took you
       places you had never screened
      before, spark from a look in this
        middleless fair city
        ventilated with cover

GRINDING HIS OWN SPECIES TOWARD EXCITABLE PROSE
  with which we'd name the streets
    your interface.

        Such simulating turns into
        a gleaned security monster calling
        down from days left as you
SERVE NEW CONTENT to
        someone come to guide
        you to a similar devotion

Someone watching you with appetite
    the face you want to save for a really big civil
        project dormant no more—it's a
            power glide, technically
        a grassy slope on which grows
        a lowly reputation that cushions us
the best weeks of the designer
tallying his crops
finessing the experimental gorges

        where you hear
            a ringing phone
            no more tropey than it should be
            a third way, middle-ear concerto
                albatross bells, all these hemispheric options
    see the anchor dropping very slowly
        faithful than the time

Officially we were meant
downtry, smiles for aught

your little country place
is so invincible, trotted
round with colored ambiance
fully recognizable as lot

your city pad is near here **STREAMING**
    REAL-TIME PARTICLES IN
    MY DIRECTION GROWN
toward us a habitat, grown for bodies
booty shifting holding tanks

why am I in the capital of strew
when beautiful and new delights
thick jostle, the certitude that one
don't work too hard to make the cultural.

4 Blood on the tracks

    The man insisted nature was a plague invented by visitors
    to stake the land by difference through thick age
        (listen to it, wag the wind by hair fallen down
            the young you tending with your legs
        the shiny suppositions of what's said on the swell)
      listen to it, the plates mended temporarily by
    magma's silent ardor

    The total absence of your mouth is wise to me, pleased
    to meet you fastly walking ravaged with soft cloths even when
          the best that all experience catch can
    her hand flew across their gentle malnutritions
          we could kiss (truism, flan, succulent
            bees on our tongues lured there by alps)
        the eyeholes patched with curfew and quite vague

   code city we are swatched in that tic tic
      rankled on the bayside sand egregious
      and she caught a willful fire next
         the fine alternatives of Weymouth Camden
     Vernal and (as the lady going out the legs
       committed to this freight
        lifted gainly for the manly cordiality
      we plug in with our flashy calisthenics)
   the heirlooms fast transmitted these keyed runes

I know you can make it to the next cave
though water rushes in quite regular to check

your breathy apoditics, your soft apologies
   wholly in my ear some version of yourself

  you cannot be, the whole soft city groaning
  in rank apology, your sweet body tending the clouds
  and tress, enamored of your task, fingers fly
    dew descending your ideas crossed against now
  wrought, now (tuck your arms in one direction
        and your head in the other sleep will come)

       the rearrangement of
      your molecules to fine-tuned
    appositives, your literals quite as sure
   as these ones.

(The brain's inside the tight box of the head
squirming like a baby dying to get out
the heart depends on darkness darkness
ticking out the syllables of the fingers click
like footsteps gathering hard beneath them
to define the eye's perimeters the tongue of language
pushes out the periscope that licks your face with
understanding while the body swivels all
its instruments toward you and we start)

        Dear co-soul how do you
          relate to the ulterior motives of our fleshly city

   Dear one rate the harboring of fugitive
     angst sailors whose every swale's intention
       moats around the curfew of your boat dear implement
    your arms and legs astound the waterspider out
       of hiding as a farmed one

                                        Dear your bare legs
                stammering out of where
                      the delicate mothers kept you near
                              the stern ones not delete?

    The stern ones kept you
near by proof
    the boat careens its naked lines
and bounce off strait
    allegiances whose colors mark
whose ends collude
    your torsos lush and rude?

Don't answer yet
the jury's out (it's hiding in the leaves and frets
it's keeping the pianos wet
it's drying out the trees with ire
and shucking pyramidal fire)
                all over city's tinder ale
                      we swig and barter wails, we try
                            our heat and fancy make
                                  our sails of mother's hair

Narrow chasm stuck inside
of mobile phones permission
        BUNKHOUSE DOORWAY
        WHERE I WAIT FOR YOU
        NEVER AGAIN SURPRISED
        THAT PLACE WHERE YOUR LEGS AND MINE
        WATCHED THE MOVIE OF OUR FATE
while muse birds and
the chimes played thoughtfully

        semaphores, the least-known
      catacombs you're walking through
          Set pieces, modernes, the actants
        all atwitter smell of smoke
     hungering for soundtracks
         from one coast to the next—it's all about
   the listeners, do you hear?

About this time the overlay of law on skin was
very pleased to greet you. About this time of truth
on guess. We hadn't made the map yet on the dove
flesh of her very streets whose treats were gliding
honey over lips on tandem eyes in windows licked.

We hadn't named on streets whose glides
were narrow or serene or barely curving
toward the water not for seen. We'd buried
though the fundamental liquid of its creasing
water down to water
RESIST US still we had the guesses
but not the thrill of skimming off
the warehouse air that rises from
the buried water seeping

    We'll start to talk in images, each word upon
          the ground re-strut (since roads are
      pyramids and buildings breathe
           like habits rusted up) the bridges built
of bones we tend, the beaches bones
ground fine (since we of water
dark and pulsing eyes are inward
firmly trenched)
                SO VIOLENCE STARTS HONESTLY
                IT SEEKS TO REACH THE BODY'S SERIOUS
                ATTENTION WITHAL THE GALL OF
                LIVING COMING OVER THE DIVIDE
                BETWEEN YOUR WORD THE SIGN
                INSTALLED THE BARRIER OF YOUR SKIN
                WHOSE BREACH WILL PROVE
                THE VIOLENCER'S MIGHT CONVEYANCE
                THROUGH OF MEANING'S TOTAL POTENCY
                        (you can no longer deny
    though delivery is totalized in the conveyance
    unfortunately that bridge once crossed can never
    sculpt again until another body's regions are
        pronounced with perfect accents plunged

    into the special corpus of a devoted listener
the teller's rage to plunder having reached the limits
John Locke meekly hoped for) that's the gift
    the murderer gives himself but only once

  compared to which the land's docility
    and mute and fragrant mirth
      dumbs down   the licking of the fiery tongue
 of Man's desire for total hooking up

The law's egregious festivals
are sipping on their liquids
not sure though they'll not say so
how to reconcile green and parch
of light and dark and make
the coastline pitch

our voices larks our mandibles to feel
and lunch we find the edges in the bunch
that looks Montana Vietnam
and underneath the sun shines down
we find the seams the earth distills and pull on them
till all falls in

The depth-charge boats were wielded
names the voices comma   same, a rain
with variant technologies
                      the earth will not
run far from you
the birds will turn and raise their plumage
                            we are under foot

   I you wait to outline
      the heretical with chalky sublimations
   of your subterranean route
       (beneath the swelling
 scenery, beneath the beat corridors carved into
    meaning's anonymity you might find
      subdivisions given away, literally
 uncarved from routes that pull fetter's emoluments)
     the same that glistened firmly
  on the glass we held between us
      you pressed textually in err

I WANT TO BE A WORKING GUEST
I WANT TO BE YOUR CANADIAN
    please, all gates are identified
      WITH SIGNS THAT RELEASE YOU
   the need arises floats on pressured sides
 the mask will fail
the lanyard cup breathes normal
syncopation when a single
reasonable citizen falls out

    statutory grown-ups with a promissory tell
  whose whisperings rise from
  their hands held up to show us
      we're not joking wave on wave
     salts gently our tear gardens, removed
        from glorious vegetables whose every verb
   and participle shape the folly
     tally of our young

     I'll hand you a delivered bird
  whilst you reward posterity with flavored
    limbs pulled down from trees designed
      to fervent yield

    Eureka glides the law in files
the magnet draws it back and forth
while parchment holds the filaments
   the hair and sand we held as
  rents
                    the earth to prove its sight
 its media language sharp   as our collusion
image fast and bright
    we'll speak in pairs, in paints
  all right

5 The Prison-house

I wish a had a process of complexity to offer but
your glam out stars are already obvious
(their beauty's pallid magnitude
not least because) the aura might be seen as
made-for-TV biopic what
we might mean by authenticity
with signs and wonders fetishized
with passion's palette
trees that tried real hard to get away
        I'M A TAPE-MEASURING EQUALIST
        SOMEWHERE OUT IN THE LOBBY TO SELL
        DELICACIES FIT IN THE CONSUMABLE
        ARCHITECTURE OF
the city of your flesh we've built at last

We've made the streets manuka burrs
      the sidewalk cracks contest
     the pretty confines of our liege
     the urgents of our bowery
      where dilettantes are precious few
the culture flags its undergirth, exposed

    I'M LOOKING FOR
    COMESTIBLES WITHIN
    THE LIGHTED SCENIC

the honey streets are sure of those
the garnet lights your languid blood
solidified, stuck up to make new furnishings
  the tripled nature of our written world
        (whose every vegetable has
      a name, whose every bird
     we hear again by virtue of
    ARRIVE DISCRETE BELONG
      though it's another song or troth
       we sinew in our docent hearts
     the world has such advantages to overwrite
    domestic urs, something to
      compare to hers)
as Trudi smites the parts of town to see who calls in pain

    The lampposts sing in feeling
naught the windows buckle out their eyes
and blind the storefront scenery
the building sides just make an oomph
and do not bend the street

    Although it cramps and roars she shakes
her ladder stick at it the honey
noncompliant shapes her legs with all
the pulse we felt as image
misadores your eyes

              A MINDLESS METTLE FELT
              IN ARC A SWEET ASPIRING
            COGNATE LARK WHOSE MELODIES
          HAVE FIT OUR EARS WITH FEALTY'S
                  FEARSOME FALLOW

   I can admonish fetter
       locks   voice-over
         togs whose swish we lack
      or feel the cramps ride up my back   narration

All this is nothing as compared with
   cabinets we ordered here
whose lovely oaken fetes will make our
  war rooms temperatures increase
         THE FEET CLAT
         BEST WHEN WE DIVEST
         OF FATTER OAKS YOU PROOF
         WHEN MILITANT INVESTMENT SPEAKS
         AS WIN AND LOSE CLEAN
           PRESS MAKE SHINE
         YOUR FILAMENTS OF LIGHT
           THE TIDY CREASING MOUTH
                  GIVES WAY
at last

nor go his smiles
toward promised wish
a gentrified suburbanite
a quintessential point of view
outmoded over the harbor

       (the hand he stretches down to you
           to pick up from the sidewalk)

mistake the smile for fundament
exchange your glasses at the very next shop
your photogenic residence
was aged from the start.
   It's time for a social history of language
but Terra plays, ear muff considerations
all a gambol. We cannot strew
the plans as clearly confident as this one
nor diffident erasures riven by

   Those waiting here have had their fun
techniques, wizardry as a way of pastoral
scrivening as honest etch
ethnohistory as a kind of platonic guest
whose every movement at the table's closely watched.

   Terra where whose face close firm
     down here his eyes as
           HE LEANS FORWARD TO GESTICULATE
   match the motions of his mouth to
         sings, he craves
     the coucou manna
        by the side of the secular divine
   tenacious living matching fire to fire

        by the side of the bird whose every song
   he craves the music to match translate
      to singe the fiery syllables
    to make the doghouse prove his point
   he takes the order of experience and shapes it
   into bread they've never seen
before, he eats.

    No songs survive from absent throats
       the hanging kite   sounds flutter

     they're leaves inside the frames
         ill trees or ilk
    a sally toward some wholly grounded
      books, the looks he gave
to substantives as finding   ears

      he holds them in
 his textual tears
  replacement soft from feeling

sitting on my head I've come to understand

from speaking, from knowing your

steel straw was stuck

      MY BRAIN AND YOUR OWN

      SUCKING HARD EXPECTANT

      MOUTH THE MAN

      THE PREGNANT ONE

          ANGRY WITH SIT

one stands and feels consequent, ready, then

the proletariat can do what it likes

rapidly through time, a ready mind

encentered of its pain

      NOT KNOWING, RIGHT THERE IN THE WINGS

          AND PLASTERS BRIGHT

I'll deal with the erasures when
they shake their willful locks
with keys made specially for harvesting
this library—shuck eaves make
lyres strew lissome veins
poured out in bloody ink
the parables and hieroglyphs put fully
in the stones and bark and long long evenings
where we hear with ears we've borrowed
from some celestial tell our argument's
cessation wet against the parturition
of the moon-made rocks

With magazines for physiognomy
>
>> this building's **HONESTLY CONVINCED**
>> it stands here for the centuries in flesh
>> to procreate its syllables to the street
>> whose passersby can barely hear, they

> open

>> the door of his eyes, they close the wringing
>> of his hands they look out slowly from the
>> seeking poses of his mouth and see
>>> a sea whose unnamed purposes surrender.

We cannot even call him names, refuted
>> by the artifice of nominals that do not close
>>> his right-to-nouness down in any form
>> he claims that for himself forestalls
>> the possibility of naming this warm building
>>> any **THING**.

The generalizing human mind becomes
a car park of experience whose signifying
chains be named Archaic
Semiology Castrato nil
Industrial Monarchy Park
closed gently for the evening
while our durable feet contract

Even when we meant it these sheaves wasted
genteel breakfasts with the fruits and descriptors
of duty, morality, and law set down instead
of being hovered by the ears of the constrictors—

    oh they're yellow orange
    blue-green, sand-borrowed plumage plans
    they're common droves fine
    calls across the sound-devouring waters
    floating into nearby space
    whose vibrant pockets keep the names
    we cannot hear without
constraining HE-WHO-WAFTS-THE-PERFUME-OF-THE-AIR
    TIE-THE-TALE-TO-SCREENS-BY-US
    WOMAN-DON'T-TOUCH-THE-GROUND

these internal negativities surround
me in a time-not-here that hovers
both before and aft that line
your gentle feet will cross
surrender to an order post hypothesis

the phoneme of the child in and out of
willful contracts that you know
a depth of naming, geologic strata
order each as Terra armor cloaking
hard upon the skin of Trudi's claims

such a thing as Trudi read HER TIRED EYES
        THE TOOL-SHOP BANTER
cleaning while the walls would tremble just beyond
the post-vocalic buttons
stud on couches
where our leather skins
slide-unslide the chains

The two great poles
are very cold, resistant
to our gleaning, we walk
with turgid limbs
the tennis slats beneath our feet
the hole below

   The metal carcass
sheath unsheathe
our open eyes like lips unlike
the stalls we separate
the point that no-one
sees the ice nor splits invented
Fort Projection task
our legs no longer clearly out
nor wither

'Let's point out the safety features of the new city'.
All exits are identified with signs that mobilize capital
The water is proprietary
floats on several sides
The thin man with his cloth
fluttering out before him gives song

   He wants his arms to be walls
   he wants his legs to be houses
   he wants the windows of his eyes
   pressurized, close to the homestead
   by the keepish posture round
      THE AMATEUR THEATRICALS WE GROW ON
      WITH OUR DIGITAL PINS SET TOWARD
         EACH OTHER RATHER THAN AWAY

We cull our social burdens one by one
with the kind of grace reserved for telling secrets
to a listener whose baby hands will trick it

all about event, our willing or unwilling selves
holding them in spades and buckets
gently near the shore of
our convenience, our farawayness shirking
self at last

      Each porous country floats
         the wreckage of its mouthy shores
  who move the sea like cucumbers in the watery
go
        take their time dinned limb to limb
      push all the people off the land and make
them body bridges loft
                the sea's alive with swim

      Thin reeds, we are
        standing slowly
      telling each other libraries

       that girl there means to join us
  see her go, this
    one joining us, stats

     he'll bring deliver
       hands on bread
  we hover here for wait

     it's gotten very quiet
    at the gates to paradise

6 Exodus

had Trudi put a thin coat of quartz vein triumph on
belatedly in fact? a bluish cast of yellow fisheyes
gamboling on the sleeves? Was that her heart?

An oblique soil produces us
a navy bloom we sashayed over
kindly, whose dialects were burr and snap
we pressed them into stone halves
of the walls we've made outlaid
beside the gentle hillocks of our vegetables
whose means were sanguine scheme
we filched into the pockets of our culture we're all lining

(with the same vein blue that caught our trolling
eye, the one we plucked out of our head
and held up heavenward to see which way
horizon's hands were sheltering this time)

We are sore from our efforts at afternoon

we are unsure of how to make the evening

which in not waiting for us has the advantage

      WITHIN A SECRET HARBOR WE KNEW

      A VERY HALCYON MOMENTOUS

          DICTIONARY TOLD US DEFINITIONS

    WE COULD fit where we demented solitude

the childhood of her lap gown on its petals

   with EVERY FAIRY LAND

  THE ONE WE MADE, the one we sought

the two we fitted round, invincible

    mortality

      appeared without a sound

Sit on my knees please
your self erasure habitats and

grievances to do like fire
eating gives us all a stomach

ache eventually you find yourself
knock-kneed on earth, the roundabouts

you drive through daily questioning
for suspects and a diatribe

accordingly we are angry at the known
AN ELSE I DO NOT LIKE

    Baroque has made this triangle
      a midland party of reluctant start
           to spilt-out   plethora 'yes it hurt'
and with primordial screws we held our hands out
to be welded to the wheels our ancestors
      paid kisses for (oh my darling
         asps and welts, come further
      don't succor me for bandly
            I must walk ideas of danger promise)
      the motto of the village whorled
       discretely in our palms whilst our relations
    build the vertical enclosure **STAND RIGHT THERE**
beside the shunt.

One might get it all oneself one's body

stretched completely round the tasseled circle

we might call a calling island without

                VOICE WE RECOGNIZE

   inside the skin

  whose circle gets pried up and wrapped

   in one kid glove to fit him, the voice

    has muffled longer claims

              THE TREES STING NATURE'S VISIONARY

              RATTLE DETACHED FROM TYPE

              FACE SEEMING

     smiling fractious for the team

       crowded at tiny tables

outside our brains we half-commit

our gleaming scales our univocal

    dominance to feed them

The body's verbs are pressed in time
        to make   to screen   to do
copse rhyming or scrape cheek refined
fleshly on the marketplace

we want we say to hide in adze or find
       before our finger   eyes
pressed down on sights
   commiserate with all we
  heave while lifting
    up our smiles all over
     each other please

the veiny architects of streets
    we play on down
   we lie in place

I'll stay here on the bishop bench

aesthetic and material

nor Europoise nor concept swell

will move me from my syllables

my body's verb appointed

to reverse itself on cue

determining set causes like

                scooter

                inward

                fragile

                door

  (the thing you pay for as the cogito

      beckons you hither, thither,

    thither you doubt your rounds

    the full set of a heel) you'll turn again

  a sennit lathe for furthering your manly stores

       of plethora, what wield in absence

         we make in shops, inside we

           further **THE FRUITION OF THE MULTIPLE**

           INCARNATE

                roses

hollyhocks   hinemoa   absence tree

we pay in kind for every one

we hide in place

We recognize consumptive glee

the mystery line makes yours to mine

devourment and Trudi's limbs

consumed in time mouth

syllables agree: come eat and make them

telescope, your ears swim fast

to shark fin boots, your aim

wedged in the concrete sand

              (but bandwidth calls we recognize

                will interfere with our assizes

          half-advanced through Trudi's eyes

        the length of yarn

          she stares encircled

        round our future power)

                    OUR FINGERS REACH THE BIRDS

                    INCREASE, THE NETS ARE RENT

                    WITH SALTED FLOWERS

                    OUR HEARTS GROW ROUNDER

                    AND A CAVERN

              opens in the middle, down which you hear

              the syllables of history's repeater.

The stoke it breathes
white picket grief
the burrs march out
steamroller lane
our blood at last appeals to you
our bones contend like sand
refuse to hear when green
speaks fast and glom it all together
its nature is inscrutable
its language topped with variants
our reason dogs roll over

Too true, think the teeth set in the skull
whose engine traceries divest their sleeves
of individual wizardry in a pose
we might call forgetting
    (excepting we can't nurture purify the scene
      we set up feeling it as natural
      embroidery, umbrellas and settees
      providing all the celebration
        stasis warrants)

Laughing silently in the jaw
line set along the water's edge
for passing feet to wedge on
those are stones whose alibis are
silence, trees whose every vein runs
deliquescent in a half-opaque scrutiny
of the scenes unfolded in your keys
something like steel plans
something like contusion metaphors
    nearby the wafting permanence
   of the trees
     and the satisfied quiescence
    of the grasses set for seeming
     port of call

in the middle Terra felt himself to be
the principal dealership in coventry arms
the sole manifest liquid in a realm of solids
core seeking heat or mandibles
touching every surface on a seek
for what to seize
       the leaves   yield
     that fellowship at   night gently
          inspecting the range of soft machinery
                   plugged in

Trudi hears them damaging minutely
the attaseconds of the glass
over her window frames
inside the ceiling
brushed with treacherous openings
for that visit—she imagines
     scores, pianos without tones, ocean heartbeat
       a whole soundscape plugged on disks whose
     frames declare the extant fits
like music, whose caws slowly
penetrate created worth.

That's when she'll willingly skin
herself on rocks and place
her ears like pearls
at the ends of swaying tree-tips
to decorate   her eyes on
the tops of passing waves
(right at the slightly foamy crests
where eyes can see)   her bones
pressed edging just inside the quite
unstable earth to make the paths
we pass through diligent for holiday

Our pinafore obligations excite
the kind of motion we convey with schism
all this more or less written on the frescoes
of the imperial bank building on the premiere
corner we thought a lot about.

Firstly, many came forward with
image abounding pioneer martyrs
with soundtracks gathering from outside
their glory was short-lived.

Though precedents were multiple still
in situ what we wanted to elucidate was
heterodox, as pianofortes are neither what we called
nor calling's reprobation here
   (according to the frescoed walls
    whose miniatures are really the amazing things
     pierced from outside with waves
      obtruding bounty that you see
       only when you and one
        another see-saw bank)
but that leaves out the words

You'd be amazed what you can see when seeing's
multiple syringe has docked it eye to eye: nothing's
rotten yet we banished wood to make this
granite face wield tiny words
confound the passing eye of Trudi
trying to make out tribulations:
>	YIELD THY STONE FACE AMMUNITION
>	FIELDS BORE DOWN
>	FOR SHAKING STILTS BREACHED
>	TOWN'S FULL WARRANT
>	 CHIMES TO BOOT—

such granularities impeached their ends immediately

Though someday there'd be hand reading
to teach us how to know
we'd lace the words with fingertips
and press them from below
>   (in the shadow of the gangplanks they read
>   granite speculations on materialism—
>   those pried from our ability to manifest
>   that language as we pass our way
>   appointment's fell logic ordering

our legs) that Trudi thinks might read
instead with rhythmic pulses slapping on the ground

7 Kit out

THE 70S HAD A GREEN HEART PLANTED IN ITS SPLEEN
start from there—majordomo of the limestone rocks
no matter how panoptic sites of learning fit our reverie
    we're substance foundered on a street
    analogous to friendship networks
    tinkering with that spleen

      or having staggered quite so far we find
    the oomph horizon pushed just past
      our feathered learning
    though we fly straight on   no walls could
          master back

        You had an unusual cornice
      manufactured in a statue   right
beside the bustling question of our metropole:

       how are we to hold the country's wedges
    in our sites? Did we ask for variance? SIRREE!
  that anyone can protest on their knees, the functional
        contact with the pavement proving they will
           centralize as fast as beating hearts can flagellate
     our guilty filing cabinet history

(here the magnets hiding their strange gliding
hands, there the concrete broken up as night
resembling the green rocks upon our stays
we whisper, reassemble, pledge ourselves)

      a physical frame 'we're going to the river, eh?'
    the question one reserves when one succumbs
  to commercial feeling, though we close up shop
   in the back of our heads
  to hide our tenant eyes from
      owning probity—

    'let us in with sprites and eyes, let us in with

  honey, we speak

      to those they make our tea

  shine bright with wine

      nor none your own chop down'

OUR ELFSTATE URGE APPEALS TO STORY WEDGES

    that one while burrow in transforming

      has to demonstrate it works   the houses lurch

        and smell of earth   the buildings heave

          volcanic ease

        the spires doom

          belief perfume

we crawl inside the furniture

        H<small>OW RIGHT YOU ARE</small>

        <small>TO DECORATE MORTALITY WITH A REAL</small>

        <small>APPORTIONMENT OF ORIGINS</small>

<small>WE EXCAVATE THE STONE CAVES OF HER HEART</small>

<small>AND IN THEM FIND A POST-SULFURIC LONELINESS</small>

        <small>TIE ME BY THE HANDS</small>

        <small>AND BURY US IN SECRET</small>

<small>HONEYCOMB HER SKYWARD EYES AS</small>

            tethered

    to the import stone   we join them—

as in a message heard by inkling children
whose magnetized responses are recorded
by the implant wares they manifest
through ranks and birds and dress
    a man writes in the known: I know
    I know, listen to my voice is the extruded
mindful trap a coinage of
    the OED (whose every volume's
modesty) whose sexual love embraced
    a new too durable machine
        I MEAN THE HEAD
        UPON MY SHOULDERS
        IS A SLOT IN WHICH IDEAS
        POUR AND OUT OF WHICH
        THEY LICK

besides, we now have early stages prepped

for colors shapes and instruments

for sites of blood and reckoning

the elders held on outward merrily

    SULK ITS SCOPE SUBCATEGORICAL

    A MISDIRECTION OF A WHOLE

of images or corpse. The nominal is very near

  is very grating bliss as text

    whose score's a lapwing swing

      agrees us all

      that terabyte's a cowl

    transfixed to lobe's insistent

    beauty wraps, arms rightfully

  in the smooth alcohol of

      preservation

  in the porous granite   promises, where someday

    3D albatrosses fly

  with people plans and   see?

    the built-in cavities of temperance!

'If you let them model
they'll relinquish real ideas
if you let them stylishly
pronounce they will
confine themselves to teacups
if you smoothly rank
their wooden ways will bevel
soft inclusions'

What did it really say?
We ground the bird bones
fecklessly and spread them smooth on stony surfaces
(and still no news) we carried sand inside our purses
and coddled it for weeks and still no messages
reached us then we captured city silt
that true stuff pushed it on the frescoes
after hours and still
no revelation.

As bad as bat dung scored
bad as cawking point-eyed birds on shore
bad as trilobites hidden in cavities bad
as anyone confessing scattered ruins
(for there are no ruins *here*)
we know the outlines are traversable
as stencil kits reviving all that energy
again it is a kind of campground
where we'll wot it seeking

        WHERE SLOWLY ON THE GROUND
        OUR TERRA PROVES THE DEEP
        DECANTING OF HIS LOVE
        FOR RETROGRADE IDEAS BOUND IN SOIL

    where you can bring your polish gear
    and set up happily, the fine sights gently
    sweeping you along for mobile ecstasies
    you activate by touching with your eyes
        (they hide when night falls gentle
        hide when no one's mouth caresses
        hide inside the ears shell caskets
        gold immobile silent wisps)

and in the morning breathing fine
you'll brush your hair back with your hand
and all arises fresh sublime
your partner blinks the darkness back
your social register accretes
the absence of your social car

you mean so well that meaning's clear confession
breaks the books you left, they split at home
their softbound clefts and all their language
spills the floor immediately absorbing more
    (because the body's flivvered up with salts
     because the limbs are loose with divigation
     because the castles will to be secured
      with notice of our lying
     next to them, whose promises and weapons
       woe betide)

All this transpires
down the mountain to flip it
on the beaches with our kin
our rellies and our sunnies
all in barbies to snicker in
our undiluted skins
(whose incense sweet
commensurate can flavor
our consumables withal unique
and tender sacks ablaze)

We come to find this menu
quite amazing, its tiny print
embedded in the curfews
of our pores (quite reminiscent of
the flecks along the bankside
flat-walled apse our granite
building calls far off where
Trudi cautious watches
her indemnity)

The workers make to recognize true value
in the added time, they slap each other's lapses
laugh the tiny beachy paradigm
whose limnal arcs make all our feet
return just where
we ought to meet

(that's underneath the fishy scales
where little midges burrow
to prove the point of flesh's doors
we open with our metaphors)

too scared to lick the open sores
that welcome tender death-in-life
OUR LAND OUR COUNTRY
AND OUR WIFE

8 The Barbie Doll Museum

Dear city code,
   The subject is an interval
     we might never make up   for false transepts
              are overage, androgen suspects
HOW ARE YOU? Our café fretwork distinguishes the time
         like promises unwept while

   I meant to make your trammeling meet
   mine in diserasure: cull the answers
      gently metagirl, she has the wedges
      ultrathin amongst the farmed-out

NICE DIMENSIONS, while handicap wives
weirded out by waiting for that newfangled
    liquefaction that the pilots will unveil
  between the circuitry

BUT I MEAN HOW ARE YOU?
(finally it was a queen who saved us
from having to claim ourselves, from
maneuvers that would force
some kind of tribal software
cause she's not finished yet)

You'll be happy to know it's been over a hundred years
since we laid waste to the concept of getting somewhere
short smiles in fleece time mean
              you'll see me without   numbers
        letters, fetters, concept road

  I can't be manly misalign in
                          water answers
    intelligent disagreement where we set aside
  dull purpose in the first place.

The next station is camaraderie
    glug glug   THEY'RE ALL REALLY JUDGMENTAL
          IN THEIR SEMAPHORES HERE, LIKE
they built their windows
    with a view toward Expectation

    You will, I know, constantly pay time
        for the transpolitical body we've yet realized
      'The only problem is the money'   some dame collapsing
          before they'd even got the bridges well-inspired

My trash is your house, benedictus
    tongue tied   around the tree in the park
trying to imagine his entrails when
      ghost at the station
implored **CAUTION REVERSIBLE LINES**
do try to keep the city in your mind when adding
       handles to the bridge to
lift it down   **NO LANGUAGE**
TILL YOU WRITE IT ON THE FACES

Dear Barbie,
Once upon a time in the west there was a female
organism principled and bare—she kept her time lags
judiciously unparcelled because she had ideas about

who would need them, who desire, she buried
the gospels to organize her heart, she used the
death rattle to sustain her sublimating energy (so

      constant that, the young man by the side
      of the road on the bicycle, the fish
      with dazzling perfume released

on the air, the round untwisted couple
ropes twanged to make sound
        replacing childhood to listen)

Count by habitats the forelocks we shake
out from the box, golden brown red curled
    startight on the shiny grey
        YOU PRESENT ME
        WITH YOUR CAKE IN MOUTH
          AND THE WARM LIQUID OF YOUR LIPS
    adventures so near as looking
      from the highway soft were sleeping
my once skated head could fall down fast again
the roadside flowers gently curling round

       The marathon is easy with   your feet like
         angels slatted on the grid   with your hands
          unsettled the rocks with   your cheek
         on the ground nuzzling   your budding go
              relations   swallows

                    The literal cups
                  at the heart pulling
                      fragmentary
                   that atomic relation
                  however multiverse

the substance of   push   treated as a subject
in its right audience, laughter   waiting for sublimity
to rescue artificially-created manufacturing
towns, conscious flaxmills, drunk fish, and belts
and pulleys round the bodies of the workmen
a former bush economy
hard to port—I mean we'll need
some ideology to love each other, right?

Dear chancery,

Everyone is very thinly walked

on razors at the edges of the sidewalk

hierarchy in heterodox uniforms, all

the keyboards the same dialectical

counters of the fantasy echo

co-existed by the humming child

learning to learn phenomenology's just

another word for companionate judgment

no worse than unproductive uniformity

I wager

The stanza's become caress, the maudlin

cloak of the sestina huddles on

the transom we're historically riding

wearing rubber sandals

to keep ourselves from the shock of the new

we've discovered meaningful physics as iterative process

BAKING AND CHURNING, BACK OF
RUN TO THIRD HILL GROUND WHEAT
AND WORK UP CREEK AND SCOURING
ALL RIGHT SQUALLY AND COLD THENCE
TO BIG STONE INTERVENING

whether a tithe or shelter, when you have a chance

I'm going to need that aesthetic expression
       CONTEXT, LINGO, ORIGIN PUSH
the out-settlers in what we've come to
understanding POETRY HAS FOUND ITS MATERIAL
     state deep surface architecture
         rather than one data fly buzzing
       on the sweat that's dripping
         over Trudi's keys she's
       nullifying on one side where
    hendecasyllables flow into the gutter

Dear seizure,

Let's take an allegorical tour of the brain
        they found the drugs in the circuitry
        unforced the number of reactions
            secretly filmic
(surfaced with mirrors you see only
the scatological leaking of your enginery
unveiled before you cover up)
                        working for the footage
            of which a replica has been   destroyed awake
           within sufficient courses where we read
              the books when it was over
        and believe our runs should forfeit recent
           experience   or at least recused
      for something fancy we can wear

When we speak to our subscribers they're scrupled
they wager each new member according to what
new campaigns must be admitted like some improvement
in the law that correlates with the same
            go who made the boat
        that day though we were going
            far from him in the ultrathin
        forgiving part of the water
      with the names to trigger
        ballot stripes or stars negotiated
           with our 3D goggles on

> HE WAS WIPING HIS TEXTUAL
> RESIDUE ALL OVER HE WAS
> FOURSQUARE WITH HIS HEAD
> PLUGGED IN THERE WAS
> ABSOLUTELY NO ROOM FOR
> THE YOUNG AQUARIUS WITH
> HIS BOTTLE SURFING

Terra lives like stanzas in burettes
(stamped with the date of shelf autonomy
beautiful exhibitionist of jars
mask filter cameral) courtesy
of the joke you make yourself
when no one's listening

He stood up and the machinery
had taken off its clothes
burrs on window cloth
(we were really on a path)

our pelts on onyx prying
(squinting against the sun
whose direct route touches us)
in permeable relatedness

The village has grown up
now, the murderer did his time
and is moved to mustering
his second life blurred passage
      lancet (through the windowpane
           quick glass)
               She pushed the button to retract
                  but without that wooing
                the trust, still finding her way
             through code with her hat and coat
         asleeve, short cut book tucked under her arm
             looking like the man he once was.

9 The film version

As a face rearranges into social meaning when it sees you
the city dilates according to your body walking
through its alleyways, umbers, vivid skiffs on prime
a tundra transit vigilant forestalled by busy

markings over its delighted waiting skin: ink this
prink it with tallies, load the streets with ideas
of their ticklish imprimatur, a designer scrawls good
distance between trajectories no one actually sees

by ocean planks, while over at the Barbie Doll
Museum we can just make out the trellises forestalled with
creeping vines I MEAN IT'S NOT ACTUAL DOLLIES BUT RATHER

the unreal substantiation of our greedy pulchritude, swooning
beaches up in flat designs, boxes of merchandise tricked out as
boxes of merchandise with the textures and colors of thick paint.

        GO ON TRUDI, MAKE YOURSELF ONE OF THEM
     handily, tweak your froth sub-line where
       we can't fit a fast conveyer since
(the ocean licks its tonsils underneath
our waiting feet, sweesh sweesh)
        we got installed however many years ago it was —
            GO ON, DON'T HOLD BACK, give yourself to
    alliance's brazier, offer something delicate
      and slim to fit between the part
   of earth that opens when implored and
the part that sternly watches
     the exceptional fact being
        taped across your mouth

GENTLE GENTLE THOU CONNIVING
it makes you lazy posing as history

when once you take the place of names
and close the door on that broad car
whose humming readiness flanks
   the cells of our primordial thick and dense
     spectacular drawing cycle:
                    take this pen and
          push it in, pull the collocation out
     set it up for fulsome wield, **SHAKE ABOUT**

     nor you have the kind of yield
       country willing to befriend dances
    in the epiderm right between
      your out and in
                  DON'T BE TIRED, DON'T BE SAD
              maxiness appeals to scrim
              cravings we have saved for us
              resting moratorium

    The languages of archeology summon
          ladders to climb—bleachers really, our limbs
             mild among them. Female figurines
       in eco-future assume the question: what do we mean
           by extinction anyway?   what
evening am I in?
             Endeavour of his self-made stones
        even luxury has its auspices (a homemade family
          woebegone to learn they've precluded non-ambition
            in the plan)
                when we came out
            like that a salt epiphany
          dreadlocks in the forenoon, pate on aft
          licking the suffix close, the car

      (our wishing well the middle of
         our lounge an altar to the license bureau, welcome
         mat for visitors shoved in to call 'create'
            a thin enticing narrow voice
            whose reeds like those we pull
            for these our worship ululations)
DIVINE ESTATE, the hills are softened
gently coruscated for the seeds
we bear, our preparation pillows
wearing lilies of the valley stems
and roses stitched on blessed hems
now henched up narrow alleys
dragged all countryward for later
fashion nation furrows

Intermission: a word walks in to a geometry
what is the word? IMBUE
yellow and red and blue
appear as colors with the words
ORANGE and BLOOD and NOSTALGIA
all over them. A ribbon falls down
assembles into STUN

concomitant: a word runs in the room: DÉSESPOIR
partial made for rivets on the soap
        life   hold the object
  any longer squeamish   without purposes
   we didn't mean to make such folly
  quotient thick ideas, nor hurt
    those waiting notions of the present

Incoming scarves are painted gay

with colors like the troves

    barbiturates we've gotten used to

      here inside the drink inside the book

  we hide to find.

A tally severance as to reach

magnanimous suppose my droves

speak forcefully, what then?

                    HEART RANCOR

                        FABULOUS INCUR

          The woman calls loudly

          hears herself repeating

            instinct suppose the teleporting

          hadn't worked this time

NOT EVERYONE'S A KIND REPEATER we reply

                to dainty elocutions we're invited

  not so familiar in flower

  stamens we get close

    our mouths I think it was

the first one hap miraculous

    as seeming fuller heartpress by the dust

wound round our mouths

Innumerable consoles elected
and both trouble time
    THEY'RE EXCAVATORS, HUMAN
     BY CONTROL
  but disappointment's just a word for WISH INSTILL
   AND YOU KNOW WHAT I'M SAYING, DUDE,
    YOU KNOW WHAT IT'S LIKE
 horizon says REPLACEMENT PARTS
  WE'VE ORDERED UP
    THEY'LL TAKE A FEW DAYS MAN SO STOP
aggrieving your exogamy
BESIDES the shore replaces all the o's
with I's the light we're eating by

for who can see when night's a fell
like stippled arrows drawn
on the anatomy of home.

She wrapped herself in red at this
and got up from the story hour
nor could re-tell the myths she heard
her ears apart the bower dark
her handle on the door pulled shut
whose sharkskin oil rigged
that bittern city

      She entrains softly by the trees
     moderate of face that passes
    reservation, here she hides
   occasion from its sister, the rains will bring
  their branches close, the soft man in the clay
 that loves him tenderly complete
the inknown city with jewels the windows
pliable moving with a neutron gaze
 through presentations made of garden
EYELIDS SHE CONCEALED WOULD BRING THE RAINS

      the hillside edges were most various
        children kneaded from the mud
   the train announced its sounds
      the mud revered light trembling, orange
         advances of the bottle men **APPARENT VISIBLE**

That is a way to manage it, the mesas different
and the same sands different and same, infolded
sutures of rupturing self-love
suckling on the answers that are cast afield
go turns his face into a molding
man his brother far away
the city cloth on hills but is it different?

One takes his barley as he finds it
one holds off shapes and fits them
feasible enlarged. Either way less subtle
more despotic the men will come
along the path bearing a heavy
sailcloth with room for more.

We have bread and also china

seeing hope enjoin our fetish sphere
emerged through cohort fitness
thinking (our banalities much to do
with cinephiles we screen) this saturated
laughter goldmine you're most charactered
within a theory chining on the sitcom
considered a game's intrepid spectacle
in a flat earth that tries real hard to get along

There are title effects in the doorway where
I wait for you conscious semaphores (because
they comfort set pieces, blithe actants
speaking gilded mouths unset)
lingering for soundtracks someone might propose
a tally to kept severance the other
as magnanimous   suppose
      outreach getting as far
  as a changed heart (of the country's fabulous incurrence)

the woman calls loudly for breakfast
hears herself repealing instinct
      SUPPOSE THE TELEPORTING HADN'T WORKED
      THIS TIME NOT EVERYONE'S A KIND REPEATER
refurbishing when   we reply
   to dainty elocutions
we're invited to   not so nice
   notion secret in flower gardens
we don't recognize nor state

  Trudi's first in the hap molecules
miraculous guess as seeming fuller
   heartpress   by the minute those
unnamable consolatories
  elect in trouble times they're ex-
cavators, human by control.

In the forgotten north they had their fullpress
implications too: a life entirely devoted
to the present yet never wanting to be forgot.
Some solve that by allegory and social type
like these cards I bought to talk with, scows conversing
        AND CHOMP CHOMP WITH THE EYES we fling out
           visible arithmetic, no one can ever find us
        under a template costing half-life
       more prehensile than we'd planned

The green shapes are comestible, the red
shapes carved for keeping moves we tally
like our breaths. The city yields a letter
temperate ghost geography gone with
rumors of its disappearance
ground that moans
beneath the walk we take

        oak shoots coming back
          out of the ground we dug them
        through, sunny day, doors open
         doomed wreck later
      congregant, supple with
          the mendacity of the brave.

   Constructed memory makes me tired
as though to marshal admiration's monogram
beguiling barrow roe
that works our language strings
of archeology among 'em
     Bask Walks Stone Ends and never complains
     YOU ARE NEEDED TO SEE THIS PICTURE

The water's tender shadows
        keep me company here as I
procure the ghosts of houses in buildings
      as I scan the absent outlines
on every corner a bot extremity
links us to the next, our eyes quiescent
          keyholes ornate transfer
as I walk the last few steps
   I find a friend of mine
might claim to be the vestiges of culture
nodes at work

That one has tied a phalanx to his head
boxed in his mind like careful scope
     next thing you know he will be worship
    (not avoiding solid walls rubbed
   into) mines where houses gain no purchase
     where the gold masks of the static principle
        meet the bare-face
     cleft   a crank of
passion sits there on the beach
displaying for all to see—it's slightly
gimpy, wishful more than kept   and without
    hiding anything I take my arms
   and turn   bones stuck up
    courteous without family
        telephone wires in dedicated liquid
  or similar trope of sporting images including
public props called reliquary
               (there she stands
  with her hair in her hands hoping for collectivity)
     stuff invested with audience location
     I hear the fragments perform tithe
     soft male voices going sacred dialect

In the interests of Goliath
or a body, she wore the red dress
   ceremonial plaster, a repeatable action
   tied around the neck of a new building
body rank preserve. Such
transactions typically leverage
     living things, dew about the mouth
(in a set of repeatable actions flanked by footsteps)
hear me out

www.ingramcontent.com/pod-product-compliance
Lightning Source LLC
Chambersburg PA
CBHW031156160426
43193CB00008B/399